D1146305

To Ann
and Steve
from

Oliver's family

Budapest, 1999. oct. 11.

Budapest

OFFICINA NOVA

Photos by PÉTER KORNISS,
with the following exceptions:

Lóránt Bérczi	41, 79
János Eifert	104, 105
István Faragó	59
András Hász	122
Károly Hemző	40, 90
Csaba Ráfael	53, 54, 69
András Surányi	60, 70

Text by MIKLÓS GYÖRGY SZÁRAZ
Layout by Zoltán Kemény
Edited by Mária Sívó

Magyar Könyvklub Budapest, 1998
Printed in
Kossuth Printing House Co., Budapest

© *Photos by Péter Korniss*
© *Text by Miklós György Száraz*
© *Translation by Gabriella Schön*

Budapest was established in 1873 by the merger of three towns: Pest, Buda and Óbuda. In the year of the unification, Buda was a sleepy town of soldiers and clerks on Castle Hill with hardly any buildings larger than one story. The empty and unfriendly Palace was deserted: no royal guests frequented its halls. Pest was larger and busier but, aside from the downtown part, it lay on the left bank in a disorganized and village-like manner. Most of its streets were uncobbled, narrow and smelly, and the City Park was infested with mosquitoes. Óbuda was nothing more than a large village. Most of its peasant citizens lived off their land and animals, produced vegetables and fruits, or were goods transporters or innkeepers. The new dwellers of the capital, these Óbuda citizens conducting a peasant way of life, spoke German, as the melodious street names indicate: Drei Herzen Gasse (Three Hearts Street), Eichkatzl Gasse (Squirrel Street) or Kleine Venedig Gasse (Little Venice Street). In summers, their coaches clattered down the narrow streets, packed high with baskets full of vegetables; they started towards the markets of Pest in the dead of night. In the autumns, the neighboring vineyards were noisy with rattles to frighten off birds, and at dawn the village shepherd collected the cows on Floriani Platz, or Flórián Square, just to drive them out through Horde Gasse, or Herdsman's Street, to the pastures of Csúcs and Üröm hills, where the sweeps of the water wells reached the sky. The Danube embankments of the newly united town were unsettled, ugly and putrid; most of the waste was carried to the washed-away embankment sides by the coaches. Citizens drank unfiltered Danube water; there was no waterworks, no sewage system. And yet, within a generation, by the turn of the century, a modern metropolis would bustle at the bank of the Danube.

Budapest is the natural geographical center of the Carpathian Basin, the one-time Hungarian Kingdom. The Danube River, running south, divides the city into Buda and Pest. Two towns, right and left banks. Two landscapes with a different character. Hills and plains. On the Buda side, the rocks of Gellért Hill almost fall into the river; Castle Hill juts out in a somewhat northerly direction. On the other side of the river, on the left bank, stretches the Hungarian Great Plain, the westernmost stretch of the huge Eastern European steppe. The sea of houses on the Pest side extending out to the horizon fits in this endlessly wide space.

The Danube has indisputably played a prime role in the establishment and development of Budapest. The big river often functioned as a border dividing two worlds. It used to be the *limes* of the Roman Empire; the eastern edge of the Frankish state of Charles the Great stretched up to its banks; and as long as no ice covered the river, the Tartar armies of Batu Khan could come only this far west. Still, it was more frequently a connecting line than a dividing line. For, since ancient times, this huge waterway winding from the foot of the Alps to the Black Sea carried, from south and west, merchants with an enterprising spirit and cultures and settlers seeking a new homeland. The land of our capital hides the archeological relics of almost every nation and culture that ever visited the Danube basin.

The first city-like settlement in the territory of today's Budapest was established by the Celtic Eraviscs. They built up their reinforced settlement on the southern slope of Gellért Hill by the middle of the first century B.C. We know their coins and nicely decorated, painted red-striped ceramics. They were good merchants and excellent craftsmen. The heyday of their settlement did not last long, because at the beginning of the first century A.D., Rome—in keeping with the will of Augustus—conquered today's Transdanubia, stretching the empire's limits "up to the banks of the Danuvius River."

If Pannonia, then Aquincum. If Aquincum, then Mediterranean sunshine, soft wind, luxury and comfort. House walls sparkling in white, plenty of grapes and blue sky. A false picture, I know, but still, it emerges in me when I say the name of "Small Rome," the seat of the province of Lower Pannonia. This is not a Mediterranean landscape, the landscape of today's Óbuda; I still cannot imagine that the red roof tiles of the Mithras Church are covered by snow. As if the weather deteriorated only later, along with the Roman city's walls. However, there was snow even then, and chilly winters. Under the mosaics of the Hercules villa, adorned with vintage scenes, lay the channels of floor heating providing warmth, just as in any other villa.

Budapest is the only major city north of the Mediterranean to have preserved such a huge, contiguous complex of Roman ruins in its heart. The heart and soul of the town was the legionnaires' camp, ringed by water ditches and walls with bastions and towers. This was surrounded by a huge town of veterans, military suppliers and merchants, the soldiers' town. The villa districts of the well-to-do bourgeoisie were erected on the hill slopes and heights. The neighborhood of the local workers and craftspeople lay to the north. The main square provided a place for the *capitolium*, the sanctuary of the empire's gods, and beside it stood the *curia* housing the assembly halls of the town's leadership. Churches, market halls, three or four public baths. Shops, inns and meat grills in the cobblestone streets of the city center. Yes, Aquincum used to be a sparkling and bustling big city. There were rows of workshops in the inner courtyards of the houses with glass windows, supplied with floor and wall heating and with wells; potters, glass-blowers, stone carvers and decorators.

And then, as Ammianus Marcellinus wrote: "The barriers on the frontier opened up, and the barbaric land poured out armed troops just as the Aetna poured its fiery sparks." After 300 unclouded years, the Mediterranean sky darkened above Aquincum. In accord with an agreement with the Huns, Rome evacuated the town at the beginning of the fifth century.

Huns, Goths, Heruls, Gepids, Longobards, and then Avars invaded the Carpathian Basin in the wake of the migration of peoples. They went further, were scattered in the fighting or merged with those coming later. The Avars were followed in the basin by the conquering Magyars. The territory of today's Greater Budapest was also of key importance for them. In the 10th century, Aquincum, today's Óbuda, became the residence of a distinguished figure called Buda; the settlement might have been named after him. The Tartar army burned down the first, ancient Buda, as well as its castle that was settled on the ruins of Aquincum in 1242. King Béla IV, fearing new Tartar incursions, founded his new seat farther south, on Castle Hill. The citizens of old Buda who moved here brought not only their belongings but also the name: thus the new town was named Buda, and old Buda became Óbuda.

In 1255, Béla IV mentioned the building of Buda as an accomplished fact: "I built a strong town surrounded by towers, with numerous apartments." In 1308, Charles Robert called Buda the capital of his kingdom, while his son, Louis the Great, built a royal palace on the southern tip of Castle Hill, separated from the town. However, this was still not the town and castle about which, a hundred years later, it would be said throughout Italy: *"Round Europe there are three pearl cities! Venice on the water, Buda on the hill and Florence on the plain..."* Buda enjoyed its heyday under the rule of Sigismund of Luxembourg and Matthias Hunyadi. Their construction work resulted in the splendid palace complex the sight of which quickened every traveler's heart and which served as a model for building the Wawel of Cracow and the Hradzin of Prague. Because Buda was really developing at an unbelievable pace. When Matthias died – that is, at the end of the 15th century – it was a big, busy city of European size and rank, radiating an Italian-inspired Renaissance culture towards Austria, Bohemia, Poland and Russia. This is how Antonio Bonfini, the Italian humanist, described Matthias's construction work: "He magnificently decorated the inner palace... he built a library filled with Latin and Greek books... Spacious dining rooms, marvelously built bedrooms... there are also richly gilded reception halls... In several appropriate places cold and warm bathrooms..." But hardly half a century elapsed before the Turkish armies of Sultan Suleiman occupied the city. In 1541 Buda, and with it half the country's territory, was absorbed into the Ottoman Empire, to remain there for almost 150 years. As early as 1555, Hans Dernschwam reported from Turkish Buda: "Houses are collapsing one after the other...they have all become pigsties... The palace has been taken over by janissaries... Stench and dirt is ruining everything."

A sad picture, even considering just the buildings, the dead stone. But think of the people! Matthias's Buda had 50,000 inhabitants even without the residents of Pest. Then, in 1686, upon the reconquest of Buda, everything was destroyed: Pest, Buda and Óbuda. Some sources wrote that, at most, 900 souls were wandering about in the territory of the three towns in 1686. Jakab Tollius visited the country in 1687. "The once-proud and glorious castle was completely shelled into ruins," he wrote in his travel notes. The Utrecht professor was unable to find accommodation on the Buda side: "I could not find any undamaged house in the town."

But, as in so many cases in the history of Pest,

Buda and Óbuda, a miracle happened again. The population of Pest-Buda was only 50,000 at the end of the 18th century. It was 150,000 in the middle of the 19th century. Upon the unification of the three cities, in 1873, it was 300,000, and just before World War I it well exceeded 1 million, including the suburbs. There was no other instance of such unbelievably rapid development among the big cities of Europe. And the rapid development beginning at the end of the 18th century was no longer propelled by Buda but by Pest.

But its beginnings were troubled. In 1686, Buda and the Turkish-occupied parts of the country were liberated not by Hungarian forces but by Austrian-led international troops. Large tracts of the once-occupied regions had become uninhabited, hundreds of villages had been wiped off the map, and the population had fallen dramatically as well. Vienna was interested in reviving the shattered country's economy but not in supporting the Hungarian nationalist endeavors. According to a Vienna chamber decree of 1688, only German-speakers of the Catholic faith were allowed to buy land in Buda. Therefore, Buda became mostly German: in 1714, only five per cent of the inhabitants of Buda Castle were Hungarian. From the beginning of the 1800s, the clerks-and-soldiers town of Buda was superseded by the merchants-and-craftsmen town of Pest as the national center of Hungarian culture. By about 1848 almost a third of the two towns' citizens were Hungarian, and by 1910, 90 per cent of the 1 million Budapest inhabitants declared themselves to be Hungarian. Certainly, Budapest became the capital and political, economic and cultural center of Hungary not merely as a result of the beneficence of the central government but, contrary to the intentions of the Austrian imperial absolutists, as a result of national awakening. The Hungarian Scientists' Society, later to become the Hungarian Academy of Sciences, was established in Pest in the first half of the 19th century. A horse-drawn tramway was in operation by 1827, and the first bridge connecting the twin cities, the Chain Bridge spanning the Danube, was finished by the middle of the century. A university relocated from Nagyszombat had been functioning here since 1874.

Genuine growth, the "miracle," occurred after the Austro-Hungarian Compromise in 1867 and the unification of the three towns in 1873. The Compromise, most of the nation felt, ended the era of oppression. And the nation, led by its capital, wanted to make use of the opportunity. Moreover, it wished to take revenge. To surpass Vienna. To show what kind of life force was bustling in the newly free nation. Budapest, the great melting pot of the nations of the Carpathian Basin, became the symbol of both national pride and Hungarian middle-class development. By 1896, the year of the thousandth anniversary of the Magyar Conquest, enthusiasm almost turned into drunken, dazed self-adulation. This nation did not want to remember its historical tragedies but only its real or imagined glory. This false view left its marks even on the capital's architecture. Our Houses of Parliament on the Danube embankment were built for a huge country stretching from the Alps to the Eastern Carpathians chasing imperial dreams at the turn of the century, and not for today's Hungary. All in all, however, a miracle remained a miracle. Because it is also a fact that between 1880 and 1900, in a matter of 20 years, a modern metropolis of 1 million inhabitants arose here near the Danube.

The Budapest of the era of unification, even if a big city, still exuded a rural atmosphere. At that time, Pest hardly stretched beyond the span of today's Great Boulevard, where a dead branch of the Danube wound at that time. Most of the capital's houses were single-story. The majority of its streets were not cobblestoned, or only partially so; peasants' coaches, aristocrats' carriages and scheduled coaches jostled along them noisily. Some donkey-drawn, two-wheel carriages also tottered on the streets of Pest, carrying unfiltered Danube water in huge wooden baskets. A big-mustached yokel walked beside his donkey, shouting: "Tónavasz! Tónavasz." That is, Donauwasser! Danube water! Around 1800, there were almost 100 Danube water vendors. Time passed them by quickly, as the growing town was in need of waterworks and a water network.

After the 1850s, the driving force of economic development was still the grain wholesalers who invested huge amounts of capital into industrial branches processing agricultural products. In the 1860s, Pest was already the center of the Hungarian milling industry, sugar and spirit production. As a result of growth in the number of agricultural machines and the development of railway construction, a number of foundries, iron and metal processing factories were established. These needed a workforce, and the mass of people pouring into the capital needed places to live. Construction progressed at a rapid pace, requiring laborers again: the process was not only self-generating and unstoppable after the unification of the three towns but actually accelerated year after year. The city's most elegant avenues (even today) were built then: Andrássy Avenue and the Great Boulevard. The Danube embankments were built, and the beautiful bridges. The multiplying traffic required an organized road network and modernized transportation. The first underground railway on the Continent was built in Budapest in 1896. Gas lighting existed here as of 1856, but the first electric lamps were lit in 1893. Budapest was a merchant city in the 1870s, while one-third of the country's industry was concentrated in the capital by the turn of the century. The huge metropolis quickly absorbed the three earlier small towns, with the exception of a few small islands.

By the turn of the century, Budapest took on its present shape. Thousands of things changed, and demolition and construction have been going on ever since; however, the general picture remained unchanged. That town is already this town. It became older and younger at the same time. But the same. In the 1930s, picturesque Tabán leading up to Gellért Hill was torn down. The decision was said to be in the interest of public health. This might be true. But it is also true that we are poorer without it. In 1945, the entire city, particularly Castle Hill, was shelled into ruins. In the 1960s and 1970s, most of the old, intimate Óbuda was pulled down. One small consolation of the demolition was that marvelous remnants of medieval buildings came to light from beneath the collapsed Baroque decorations of the ruined dwellings of the Castle. And, in Óbuda, wherever the drill hit the ground, the ancient ruins of Aquincum came to the surface.

The city is continuously changing. Old buildings disappear and people, colorful figures of the streets, disappear too. By the turn of the century, the Danube water retailers working on the streets of the old city disappeared, along with the oil-selling women with their black jugs. The Serbs selling honey candy, the Transylvanians selling "pine water," the Bosnians in their red fez and baggy trousers, the Swabian milk-maids – they also disappeared. Some vanished because time passed them by, others because they were left outside the country's borders after the partitions imposed by the Treaty of Trianon. The only ones remaining were those who had always been and would always be here: streetwalkers, pickpockets, beggars and those playing three-card trick. And, of course, the ice-cream vendors and balloon sellers. But the sidewalk has become more colorful in the last decade or so. The chestnut roasters are reappearing, along with people selling corn on the cob. And from Transylvania the grandchildren of the pine-water sellers returned to the streets of their one-time capital to offer homespun, stitched goods, painted ceramics and wicker baskets to passers-by. The sidewalk artists are busy again: street organ players and other musicians, and aspiring artists drawing on-the-spot portraits. Elderly ladies with bouquets of flowers, young Gypsy women with green peppers and sports shoes and leather jackets that are more original than the original.

Only we are getting older, the dwellers of the city. The city itself, if it is a living city, is not getting older; it is only changing. Its old quarters are renewed as the newer ones deteriorate. Streets and buildings disappear, and from beneath their debris yet older ones emerge. We, the dwellers, die, and the city is not reborn in our children and grandchildren but becomes different. But the pictures in this volume speak more vividly than any words about this constantly changing, ever-developing city.

Finally, one more thought. It is not my own. One of Budapest's more perceptive chroniclers said, and I quote: "To write about Budapest's history without speaking of Hungary's is as much a self-delusion as recounting the past of Paris without the history of France." However, he adds, the history of a capital is more or less a cross-section of what has happened in the country.

1. *The Danube embankment on the Buda side, Hotel Hilton on Castle Hill, Fishermen's Bastion and Matthias Church*

When I pronounce the word Budapest, it is the Danube that comes to my mind first. The wide river rolling through the city of 2 million. Everything else – the Fishermen's Bastion, the Freedom Monument, the Houses of Parliament – these are only accessories, scenery.

2. Margaret Bridge, designed by the French Ernest Gouin, viewed from Buda
3. The Buda bridgehead of Elizabeth Bridge, with the monument to Bishop Saint Gellért
4. The panorama of Pest with the Chain Bridge, from the Royal Palace in Buda

5. *Elizabeth Bridge spans the Danube with a single, 290-meter arch*
6. *The stairs of the Pest side of the Danube embankment are a paradise for fishermen, daydreaming lovers and students preparing for exams*

"One can see few panoramas as noteworthy as the one these two towns, Buda and Pest, can boast.
A wide river, the Danube, divides them; however, in reality they form two parts of a single city." In 1837, when the Russian traveler Prince Diemidov put these lines down, Pest-Buda had only a single pontoon bridge: in the middle of it, Saint John of Nepomuk stood in a golden cloak with tin stars above his head and an ever-burning candle at his foot.

5

6

Then bridges were built one after the other, and the unity of the twin cities became reality. The first was, the grand old Chain Bridge.
The idea of building it originated with István Széchenyi, the reform politician said to be the "greatest Hungarian."
Its festive opening was in November 1849.

8

9

7. *Elizabeth Bridge viewed from the side of Gellért Hill. The new, streamlined cable bridge was built onto the pillars of the old, Secessionist bridge*
8. *Szabadság (Freedom) Bridge, with the Gellért Bath in Buda in the background*
9. *The lions of the Chain Bridge were carved by a Lőcse-born sculptor, János Marschalkó*

15

With its classic lines radiating calmness and strength, with its triumphal-arch-like pillars and stone lions, it became one of the city's symbols. Second was Margaret Bridge, slender in the French style, commissioned in 1876. The bridge bends sharply in the middle, at the southern tip of Margaret Island; thus the pillars of the two bridge halves turn against the river's current with their edges in both Danube branches. With its weighty, raw iron structure, Szabadság (Freedom) Bridge, which once bore Franz Joseph's name, was perhaps meant to represent the development of Hungarian heavy industry in the ecstasy of 1896, the thousandth year of Hungarian statehood. If the Chain Bridge is the triumphal arch of the Reform Era, then Elizabeth Bridge is that of Hungarian Secession: when commissioned in 1903, it was the largest single-span suspension bridge in the world. In the winter of 1944-45, the Germans blew up Budapest's bridges; Elizabeth Bridge was rebuilt in 1964 in a simpler, more modern form. The elderly of the time accepted the new bridge, but they never grew to love it.

10. *Margaret Bridge viewed from Pest*
11. *Elizabeth Bridge: a bird's-eye view*
12. *Szabadság Bridge, which once bore the name of Emperor Franz Joseph*
13. *The Chain Bridge, with its Classicist, triumphal-arch-like pillars, became one of Budapest's symbols*

14

14. *The church of Tabán from the Gellért Hill*
15. *Castle Hill with Hotel Hilton and Matthias Church. In the background the ribbon of the Danube, Margaret Bridge, Margaret Island and Pest on the other side*

15

Margaret Island. It was also called Rabbit Island, Our Lady Island and Palatinus Island. A huge green spot in the heart of a bustling metropolis. At one time it could have been called the island of monks. In the 12th century, the Premonstratensians built a church and a cloister here, and in the following century, King Béla IV erected a convent for Dominican nuns here. Nowadays, mostly those wishing to swim and jog, strolling lovers, and grandpas and grandmas taking care of small children frequent the place, the island of calm and peace.

16. The northern tip of Margaret Bridge, the Water Tower and the Open-Air Theater in the front, Árpád Bridge and Óbuda Island in the background
17. Small warm-water lake in the rock garden. "In wintertime, one can often see steam rising into the air," noted an 1872 guidebook to the island

King Béla sent his daughter Margaret,
for whom the island is named,
to the Dominican convent during the Tartar
invasion and offered her as a servant to the
Virgin Mary. The princess took her nun's oath
in the convent of the island before the altar
of her own cousin, Saint Elizabeth of Hungary.
Miracle-working Princess Margaret, who lived
a saintly life, could stop the flood of the
Danube and could calm the storm, but was
unable to prevent the destruction of the
island's churches. In the Ottoman era, the
churches and cloisters of the
Premonstratensians, Dominicans and
Franciscans were destroyed; only their ruins
are visible today.

18. *The island's promenades are deserted in wintertime;
only a few intrepid nature lovers and brave joggers appear*
19. *The Premonstratensian Church from the 12th century,
the reconstructed Saint Michael Chapel*
20. *Attila József's bust on the Művész (Artists') Promenade*

19

At the end of the 18th century,
the island was taken over
by the palatines, the Hungarian
Habsburg princes. They leveled
out its hilly land. Palatine Joseph
planted sycamore trees
beside the native elm and oak
trees and built a marvelous rose
garden. According
to contemporary writers,
the island turned into
a miraculous garden; they called
it a "replica of paradise."
The first Pest-Buda regatta
started from here in 1843,
and the Prince of Wales, later
to become Edward VII, attended
the 1873 competition.

18

20

21. *The Saint Michael Chapel in summer*
22. *Silent lovers sit on the island*
23. *"Rabbit Island" bathed in autumn colors*

P arliament, built in a Neo-Gothic style, stretches haughtily along the Pest side of the Danube embankment, as if it wished to counterbalance the Buda Palace or even all of Castle Hill. It is true that the building, rising on land reclaimed from the Danube during the construction of the embankments, in the place of the once-neglected Tömő Square, is really a substantial building. With its close to 700 rooms, 268-meter length, 123-meter width and 18,000-square-meter base area, it would not fail as the parliament of an empire. In 1885, when construction started, and in 1904, when it was finished, the building still had a country to match it, even if not an empire but three times the size of today's Hungary. And the country was preparing for the festivities of the thousandth anniversary of the Magyar Conquest. The Parliament's cupola is 96 meters high, not by chance, it is said, but to symbolize the millennial year, 1896.

24. *The Neo-Gothic building of Parliament was built on the Danube embankment with a splendid view*

Anyway, the respectable Estates of the Realm were really in need of a more appropriate edifice at the turn of the century. For even in the 16th century they gathered under the open sky and then held their sessions in the coronation city, Pozsony (now Bratislava, Slovakia). When they moved to Pest in 1848, there was not yet a suitable building. Well, the Parliament building, designed by Imre Steindl, became one. One of the most impressive buildings of the country was put in a place it deserved. A contemporary report noted: "The magnificent building requires that it stay free and that care be taken to ensure an environment matching its dignity." One old-time storyteller of Pest-Buda wrote: "Imre Steindl was born in Pest; his father was a respected jeweler. The son presented a jewel to his native city that sparkles most beautifully over the queenly body of the Danube."

28

25. *The designer of Parliament on the Danube embankment might have been influenced by the building of the British Parliament on the bank of the Thames* 26, 27, 28. *Painted sculptures, marble, rich gilding. Corridor details in Parliament building*

29. The Pest bridgehead of Elizabeth Bridge
with the Downtown Parish Church and downtown Pest
30. Kossuth Lajos Street, with one of the twin Klotild palaces in front

The he largest horse markets of Hungary are held in the town of Pest. Here one can buy as many as 2000 horses, wrote Knight Bertrandon de la Brocquiére, the lord high steward of the Prince of Burgundy, Philip II, in 1433. Today one can buy dream cars and old wrecks, for that matter, in the city of Pest, even as many as 2000. But one can also buy antique furniture, old gas pumps from Texas, exquisite French gowns or the organ of a village church—and perhaps even horses. Pest, older than its counterpart Buda, still young forever. Always the same: a single, huge market. Even its first dwellers, the Ishmaelites, who settled in the Pest castle in the mid-10th century, made their living on trading.

Abu Hamid al Garnati, a Granada-born Moor, wrote about the slave market of Pest in about 1150: "A nice woman servant costs 10 denars... I also bought one, she was only 15 and more beautiful than the full moon; her hair and eyes black, her skin white as camphor." A real tradesman, taking into account not only the beauty of his commodity but the practicality as well: "She could cook, sew and count." As Reinhold Lubenau put it, the Turkish Pest of 1587 "was inhabited by rich, aristocratic merchants from whom one can buy anything he wants."

31. *The Naiads' fountain on Ferenciek Square, built in 1835*
32. *The Secessionist facade of the Parisian Courtyard*
33. *One of the Klotild palaces from behind the gate of the Parisian Courtyard*

34. *View from the Chain Bridge end of the Danube Promenade.*
Víziváros on the other side, the Castle Hill with Hotel Hilton above
35. *The "Small Princess" sculpture on the railing of the Danube Promenade*
36. *The eternal favorite of children: pouring, gurgling water.*
One of the water-spouting lions of the fountain on Vörösmarty Square

34

The famed Danube Promenade of Pest—the walkway for pipe-smoking dandies and the big stage for ostentatious ladies—matured into elegance by the turn of the century with its row of hotels and inviting terraces of cafés. The famous, now-demolished hotels of old times—Hungária, Ritz, Bristol and Carlton—have now been replaced by new, massive hotels, and the marvelous panorama from the promenade has not changed either. Across the Danube, to the south, the rocks of Gellért Hill rise, and right in front is Castle Hill with the Royal Palace.

36

37. *Váci street in the City*
38. *Vörösmarty square—the great scene of street musicians, portraitists and mimics*
39. *A concert in front of the monument of Mihály Vörösmarty*

The tiny area between Elizabeth Bridge and the Chain Bridge is the downtown of downtown Pest. Hotels, travel agencies, elegant shops and department stores cluster here. The words of the Russian traveler Bronevsky, who walked here in 1810, still hold true: "I saw shops richly packed with silver, paintings and sculptures, crowded cafés and restaurants at every step."

The Downtown Parish Church is the only building remaining from medieval Pest. It was almost pulled down upon the construction of Elizabeth Bridge. And then, as the stalls and booths glued to the building were wrenched off, the beautiful Gothic building suddenly presented itself. Only a few relics remained of the 12th-century, tiny Romanesque church onto which it was built. Gothic style and Baroque mix on the exterior of the three-nave church of today. The Ottomans turned this church too into a mosque; a mihrab booth preserves their memory today.

*42. Secessionist mosaic on the facade of
a building on Szervita Square*
43. Glass facade of a modern building on Váci Street
*44. A tower of the Dohány Street synagogue.
The building, with its Byzantine-Moorish style,
is one of Europe's largest synagogues*
*45. The allegorical sculptures of the facade of the
Vigadó, built in the early 1860s*

44

42

43

If we say Pest, we think
of the line of apartment houses
and huge public buildings, balconies
and loggias, Herculeses carrying real
or fake loads, columns, cupolas,
the ocean of small towers—
Eclecticism. Styles merge: Antiquity,
Renaissance and Baroque,
then Neo-Romanesque, Neo-Gothic,
Neo-Baroque. By the turn of the
century, Eclectic Pest "devours" its
classically calm, cool former self.
And, today, this Eclecticism is the joy
of tourists and the pride of the Pest
citizen.

46. *The sculpture of Saint Stephen, sculpted of Carrara marble, stands on the high altar of the Basilica*

47. *The four Evangelists and the 12 Apostles guard the external niches of the cupola and the external arch of the apse, respectively*

48. *The magnificence of the building can be appreciated from a bird's perspective as well*

The Saint Stephen Parish Church, popularly known as the Basilica, is Budapest's largest church. The partly Classicist, partly Neo-Renaissance church was built on a piece of land with a peculiar past. Until 1810, Pest's "gladiator arena," the "Hecc (Prank) Theater," operated here. In 1793 the Dresden-born count J.S. von Hoffmannsegg saw ox fights, dog and bear duels, wolf, wild boar, tiger and leopard fights here. The "master of the prank," as the count wrote, "wore a sleeveless shirt and leather trousers; his round hat was decorated with green feathers." Was it because the soil soaked with the dead animals' blood took revenge, or perhaps because the foundation was bad? The huge cupola of the church then under construction collapsed with a mighty crash on January 22, 1868. The troubled construction work was not finished until 1905.

49. *Szent István Boulevard at sunset*
50, 51, 52. *When apartment houses were still built with care. Staircases of houses in Apáczai Csere János Street and Kossuth Lajos Street*

52

50

51

In the mid-19th century, Pest hardly stretched beyond today's Great Boulevard, where a big dead branch of the Danube was winding at that time. The town planners of the later era toyed with the idea of building a wide channel suitable for shipping here, instead of today's Great Boulevard. Had it happened this way, no buses would rumble down the boulevard; instead, sightseeing water-buses would ply on the water of the curved channel among the apartment houses. In designing these houses, the architect's primary task was to impress the visitor right upon entry by the rich ornamentation of the gate, the entrance hall and the staircase, in order to reflect the prestige of the owner and tenants.

The Opera House on Andrássy Avenue became the home of world-standard performances and artists shortly after its opening in 1884, and it has managed to preserve its world fame to the present day. In 1873, in the year of the unification of Pest, Buda and Óbuda, toothless old women wailed on Hermina Square; then the Neo-Renaissance building with excellent acoustics and breathtaking beauty was built to replace the flea market. It hosted such famed conductor-directors as Gustav Mahler and Otto Klemperer. The opening gala performance was honored by the appearance of the "administrator-emperor" Franz Joseph as well, so the premiere of Ferenc Liszt's fairly anti-imperial "Hungarian King's Song" composed for the occasion was canceled. On the walls of the Opera on Andrássy Avenue, adorned with sculpted ornaments and frescoes, the rigid and slow-witted Habsburg disappeared, but the emperors and princes of music, Liszt, Wagner and Verdi, remained.

53. *The stair hall with the marble main staircase of the Opera House*
54. *The building, with excellent acoustics, is one of Europe's most beautiful theaters*
55. *The building, resembling the Vienna Opera House, is adorned with sculptures of muses*

55

Plaster dreams, cheap facades, pseudo-
cupolas on a single building—a world
of scenery. But if it is downtown, the Small
Boulevard, Andrássy Avenue, the Great
Boulevard or the multitude of streets and
squares, an entire city, there is some
inevitability and some genuineness in it.

56. *Mosaic-decorated corner on József Attila Street*
57. *Detail of a painted facade on Kodály Körönd*
58. *Eclectic facade on Károly Boulevard*

L ook at its sculptures and you know everything about a town. But even their absence is revealing. Old Pest-Buda had only a few sculptures: the Ottomans demolished almost all of them. Evlia Chelebi, the Turkish traveler, admired the sculptures and fountains of the Buda Palace in 1663: "There is a beautiful big basin of white marble" on the square of the Kizil Elma Palace of Buda. "… Pure water pours into the marble basin round and round from the white heads of frightening, vicious-looking goblins." The Renaissance sculptures were destroyed, and 18th-century Pest-Buda was the city of the charmingly clumsy Saint Florians and Saint Johns of Nepomuk. And, certainly, sometimes the fate of a sculpture, like that of a person, may take peculiar turns. The golden-cloaked Saint John of the old pontoon bridge gathered dust in a corner of the Víziváros Church after the bridge was demolished, then it set on the river again: it became the protecting saint of a grain-shipping tanker, and then it got lost. One of our first public square sculptures, the early-19th-century Naiads' Fountain, also wandered around a lot; it even turned up in Kőbánya until it finally found its original place, Ferenciek Square, in 1976. But even giants sometimes move around. The Danubius Fountain, whose huge base was carved from a single stone weighing close to 100 tons, originally adorned Kálvin Square and was moved to Elizabeth Square only in 1959.

59. *A female figure of the Danubius Fountain on Erzsébet Square. The male figure atop the fountain personifies the Danube; the three female figures symbolize the main tributaries of the Danube: the Tisza, the Dráva and the Száva*
60. *Raincoat after rain… The somewhat clumsy Saint Florian, situated on the external wall of the sanctuary of the Downtown Parish Church, was sculpted in 1723*
61. *Eclectic "body-builders" on the facade of a building on Andrássy Avenue*

51

62. *The corner cupola of the Museum of Applied Arts*
63. *Cream-puff ornaments carved of stone*
64. *Looking for the beautiful lady of the great Indian mogul or Sheherezade... The great hall of the museum*

If there is such a thing as specifically Hungarian architecture, then Secession qualifies. Its most beautiful example is the building of the Museum of Applied Arts on Üllői Avenue. Even its exterior is captivating. Its Eastern-style cupolas, lace-decorated walls, colorful burnt Zsolnay tiles and majolica ornaments immediately attract the eye. From the entrance it looks like a huge cake made of snow-white meringue. It is bright, airy, friendly and improbably light. Modern steel structures and plenty of glass—we still search for Harun al Rashid and Sheherezade. Ödön Lechner—Mackintosh's and Gaudi's Hungarian brother—combined Arabic and Indian architectural elements with Hungarian folk art motifs in a masterly manner.

64

62
63

53

65. The courtyard of an apartment house on Szentkirályi Street
66. Semiramis's hanging garden—in two square meters. A balcony in Józsefváros
67. A fountain with sculpted figure in the courtyard of an apartment house on Vámház Boulevard
68. The building housing the Institute of Geology is a nice example of Hungarian Secessionist architecture

66

65

The Eclectic—Neo-Renaissance, Neo-Gothic or Neo-Baroque—facades often hide desolate courtyards with iron drainage pipes in the middle, buttressed round corridors and temporary shelters. But we are often surprised when a doorway with falling masonry hides tiny "Gardens of Eden" with wall fountains, sculptures, trees and flowers.

67

69. *The National Museum, with a statue of the great poet János Arany*
70. *Stained-glass window with the portrait of Lajos Kossuth in the*
Gresham Palace on the Danube embankment
71. *Sándor Petőfi's statue on Március 15 Square*

69

KOSSUTH LAJOS

70

The National Museum: at once the symbol of Pest's development, the Reform Era, Hungarian culture and the 1848-49 Revolution and War of Independence. The Hungarian crown jewels are kept here. The building that best exemplifies our Classicist architecture. In 1837, when its construction began, the place was surrounded by tiny huts, coaches sank in mud and manure up to their axles; and drunken coachmen and swineherds came to blows in neighboring Two Pistols Inn. Within 10 years, it was surrounded by aristocrats' palaces.

71

72

72. *Archangel Gabriel symbolizing victory atop the column of the Millennial Monument*
73. *The mounted sculptures of the seven conquering Magyar chieftains, with Prince Árpád in front, at the foot of the column*
74. *Heroes' Square; Műcsarnok (Palace of Exhibitions) on the left, the Museum of Fine Arts on the right*

Andrássy Avenue, the most elegant avenue of the city, leads into Heroes' Square, which radiates dignity; the high column of the Millennial Monument stands in its axis, and the sculptures of Hungarian rulers, our Transylvanian princes and the men who distinguished themselves in our wars for independence stand in the rounded, arch-shaped column hall. Tourists bustle on the polished-stone square, cameras click, but the genuine "owners" of the place are skaters and skateboarders and manic bicycle acrobats doing handstands or wheelies.

73

74

58

75, 76. *Vajdahunyad Castle with the*
Városliget (City Park) Lake

75

City Park stretches behind the big square.
It was once a sandy, watery, marshy land.
Its names are nice examples of change: it used
to be called Oxen Path, Game Park, City
Forest, and Amusement Garden. It was actually
developed by the grand festivities of the 1896
millennium. That was quite a time!
The predecessor of today's Amusement Park,
the Ancient Buda Castle, was built; then came
the harem of the pashas of Buda, the mosque
and the Turkish bazaar. Indian dancing girls
wiggled their hips, dervishes whirled, and
Indian fakirs, the Barnum circus, French fire-
eaters and Italian sword swallowers joined in.

76

Vajdahunyad Castle was also built
for the 1896 commemoration. Its designer had
the task of presenting all the architectural
styles to be found in Hungary in a single
building complex on the tiny island
of the City Park Lake. The mix was a fair
success; the Park would be almost empty
without the castles picturesque contours.

*77. Vajdahunyad Castle is a picturesque mix of
castles, palaces, towers and churches of
Transylvania and the former Upper Hungary
(now Slovakia)*
*78. The tympanum of the Eclectic-Classical
Műcsarnok*
*79. Anonymus's sculpture in City Park.
The anonymous notary of King Béla III
wrote the Hungarians' chronicle at the end of
the 12th century*

80. *The cupolas of the Széchenyi Bath*
81. *The ferris wheel in the Amusement Park*
82. *A relic of the Amusement Park, the Secessionist carousel*

80

81

The area, adorned with huge sycamore trees, has been a genuine city park for almost 200 years. Museums, restaurants, a circus, an amusement park, zoo, skating rink and a bath for all those who wish to take a rest here or want to enjoy themselves or laugh.

82

83. *The signboard of the*
Gundel Restaurant in City Park
84. *The Gerbeaud patisserie on*
Vörösmarty Square
85. *Venetian chandeliers,*
twisted marble columns, bronze sculptures
and galleries—the New York Café

Gundel, Gerbeaud, New York. Three names from the "happy time of peace." Three big names. The Gundels are a family of restaurateurs with a history going back several generations; by now the name has become intertwined with the restaurant in City Park. In 1939 the New York Times wrote in connection with the American "guest appearance" of Károly Gundel's cuisine: "Gundel's restaurant is better propaganda for Budapest than a shipload of brochures." Born in Geneva, Emil Gerbeaud took over the famed Kugler Patisserie on today's Vörösmarty Square in 1884. His patisserie, with its French taste and atmosphere, is the favorite place of well-to-do old ladies of Pest and tourists. The New York Café was opened in 1894. "The most beautiful café in the world," it was called at the time. Surely, it was and remained the most beautiful in Pest and Hungary at least. And not simply a café but a piece of our literary life: it was once the workplace, prison, dining room and bedroom of poets and writers.

66

illy Buda.
The shady row of chestnut
trees stretching along the
Danube embankment, and (lest
we forget) the Buda
promenade. And the distant
panorama, the softly rolling belt
of hills hugging the city
on the right bank. Houses
sprouted up almost everywhere
along the high hills, but green
spots still exist, grassy clearings,
leafy forests or rock walls
sparkling in white. Hűvösvölgy,
Zugliget, Pasarét, Óbuda,
Krisztinaváros and Víziváros.
All of them small towns in the
big one. It is precisely this
diversity and variety that
captures the wonder of Buda.

86. *The towers of the Saint Anne*
Church in Víziváros, with
Margaret Bridge and Pest in the
background
87. *The Tabán Church in Buda*
Castle. A detail of the gate tower
of the big bastion on the left, and,
from a distance, Elizabeth Bridge
88. *A house on Lovas Street*
viewed from the castle wall

89. *One of our oldest baths, the Király (King) Bath in Víziváros. The old Hungarian bath was rebuilt by Sokoli Mustafa, the pasha of Buda, in the mid-1500s*
90. *Gellért Bath, once nicknamed "Muddy," could today be called "Shiny"*
91. *Classicist gate, glassed-in Empire courtyard, Turkish cupolas and pools—in perfect harmony in the Király Bath.*
92. *The Gellért Hotel and Bath*

90

This is how Knight Betrandon de la Brocquiere praised the baths of Buda in 1433: "There are very nice warm baths outside the walls." Lubenau, the physician of Königsberg, remarked about the spring in the bath of Gellért Hill in 1587 that "even a pig could be cooked in it." Evlia Chelebi knew of eight "perfect" thermal waters of Buda in 1663—he even tried them all. Buda, Óbuda and Margaret Island were also sites of baths: only the bathers—Romans, Hungarians, Turks—changed.

93. *The statue of Bishop Saint Gellért on the side of Gellért Hill;
in the foreground, the Danube, Elizabeth Bridge and Pest
on the other side*
94. *A sculpture group symbolizing Buda and Pest above
the water reservoir on Gellért Hill*
95. *Sixteenth-century Turkish gravestones on the side of Castle Hill*

It is as if the bishop who died a martyr's death in 1046 asked a blessing for Pest and the bridge, that is, the marriage of the two towns. The king and young princess of the allegorical sculpture group—Buda and Pest—reach out for each other, but in vain: the Danube divides them like an abyss. Perhaps both interpretations are true. Perhaps Budapest's greatest attraction lies in the landscape and architectural contrast of the two banks. A varied, hilly Buda side and Pest in front, vanishing in the misty horizon, flattening out into the huge Great Plain.

95

96-99. *Torso sculptures and gravestones of the Roman era in the Aquincum Museum*

Archaeologists found a wealthy woman's grave on the grounds of the Gross and Weiss hat factory in Óbuda when it was torn down in 1912. Golden earrings, silver hairpins and a necklace with an inscription in Greek on its glass medallion: "Whatever they say, I don't care. Just love me, it will be to your benefit." And a worn horn comb with the inscription: "Vivas felicitas!"—live happily.

100. *The Rococo building of the one-time White Cross Inn on Batthyány Square*

101. *The building of the Sipos Fishermen's Garden on Óbuda's Main Square*

102. *The oval-shaped building of the one-time Silk Mill was built in 1785. In it, Apotino Mozzocato, the elderly Italian silk industry expert, "taught people silk milling and weaving"*

The old houses of Buda have a fairytale-like history. Carnival celebrations and theater performances were held in the gala hall of the one-time White Cross Inn at the end of the 18th century. The romanticism of Buda gave rise to some risqué stories: fleeing from the chambers of Venice, Casanova would court the nice innkeeper woman, and Empress Maria Theresa and the stylish Count Grassalkovich would rendezvous here. In fact, Emperor Joseph II stayed here in 1783 and 1784, and in 1838 it was so flooded that boats plied the water under its basket-arched gate. Today, no postal coaches could possibly start from the gate towards Vienna, Kassa (Kosice) or Kolozsvár (Cluj), as the street level of the one-time Bomba (Bomb) Square has risen up to the window of the building.

The Matthias Church and the Fishermen's Bastion. Fin-de-siécle fairytale world. An Eclectic Disneyland. The imitation of Gothic and Roman architecture that never was. Picturesque opera scenery at a panoramic site, in the center of Castle Hill.

This was the intention, realized in full. Church, bastion and a modern hotel in a single, effectively composed unity. Not oppressing but expressing the genuine historical core.

103. *The view of the Matthias Church from the Danube with the Fishermen's Bastion*
104. *The Hotel Hilton was built atop the remnants of the one-time Dominican Church and cloister*
105. *The statue of King Saint Stephen, with the southern tower of the Fishermen's Bastion behind it*

Matthias Church, Church of Our Lady, Coronation Church. Its history is the history of Buda as well. King Béla IV began to construct it after the 1241-1242 Tartar invasion. In 1302, Buda excommunicated the pope from here. Charles Robert was crowned here in 1309. A relic of European fame, the body of alms-giving Saint John, sent to Matthias by the sultan, was also put here. Yet, in a matter of hardly 40 years, the relics had to be rescued—from the very same donor. After 1541, for almost 150 years, the church's name was Suleiman Djami or Eski Djami, Old Djami.

107

108

106. *Aerial view of Matthias Church*
107-108. *The Neo-Gothic external ornaments of the church*
109. *The nave and high altar of Matthias Church*

109

110. *Wings of stairs of the Fishermen's Bastion under the parapet*
111. *The Trinity Sculpture with the old City Hall of Buda*
112. *Tárnok Street in wintertime lights. In front, consoled*
apartment houses with arcades from the 14th century

Since 1686, the year Buda was recaptured, plague had been a constantly recurring "guest." Buda's citizens took an oath to raise a statue of Trinity; it was unveiled in 1713. The figures of saints kept multiplying at the foot of the statue year by year, and then, as the danger of epidemic passed, the sculptures were sold one by one (ungrateful posterity!). More than one sculpture of a protective saint wandered to the gardens of Hűvösvölgy villas to serve as an ornament there.

The Castle in summertime:
a bustling hive. Restaurants,
bars and confectioneries,
as if awaking from their winter
sleep, stretch out from their
cool arches onto the sidewalks.
Those who live off tourists
appear here: street musicians,
organ players, landscape
painters. The funny acts around
the Fishermen's Bastion:
the motionless "bagman,"
the knight armored in
cardboard bowing for money.
In autumn the streets and
squares become quiet, and the
Castle turns into itself again, a
sparsely populated small town
with a medieval street structure.

113. *Fortuna Street, the tower of*
the Evangelical Church and the
National Archives
114. *In summertime, the small*
bar extends onto the sidewalk
115. *Horse-drawn coach jostles*
along the cobblestone street

116

118

117

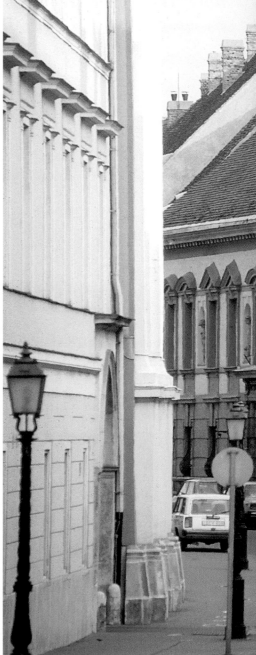

116, 117, 118, 119. *Houses in the Castle District hide stone carvings, saints or town-protecting sculptures in the niches of their facades*
120. *Eighteenth-century Zopf and Baroque in Úri Street*

120

Úri Street. The only street in the Castle that stretches the entire length of the quarter. The ground plan of its development and its roadpath are medieval. Its southern section used to be inhabited by German cloth traders; its name was Kalmár or Posztómetsző (Merchant or Cloth Cutter) Street, while its Hungarian section was Mindszent (All Saints) Street. The Buda branch of the Fugger bank house functioned here in 1532. After 1541, the Ottoman financial office moved here. The Ottomans have not given up the Castle even today: the Turkish Embassy is to be found here.

W alking in the Castle District, we cannot find any streets intact in their medieval form, not even a single house. Still, if we glance into the gateways, the tiny courtyards, the once well-to-do town reveals itself to some extent, even if modestly. Let's mention just one distinctive feature of the houses of the Castle District: a row of 63 Gothic sitting nooks came to light in 33 gateways from beneath the falling masonry in World War II. A well-known spectacle in Gothic churches. But what are these rows of nooks in Gothic style, with semicircular or trefoil arches, doing under the gateways of middle-class houses? Benches for juicy gossiping? Perhaps some of the merchant houses had their shops under the gateway? Was it a simple case of flaunting one's wealth? The answer remains a mystery.

122

124

121. *Cobblestoned passage in the Castle District*
122, 123, 124. *"Small-town" courtyards: arches, ascending Gothic cellar stairs, consoled corridors, small sculptures*

20 Országház Street. An Italian-type Gothic apartment house built in the late 16th century. Its builder was almost certainly an Italian settler in the one-time Italians' Street. There is a well in the house's cave cellar, and its shaft goes through the basement and the floor; the tenant could pull up water in buckets to the floor right through the 17-meter shaft. Its first tenant after the Turkish occupation was Johann Baadter, a carpenter and gun-maker. At the end of the 18th century, first Thomas Hueber, the town's locksmith, then János Nickli, a butcher, lowered their buckets to the cool water of the cellar's well.

125, 126, 127. *Basket-arched gates and windows in the Castle District*
128. *The consoled, trefoil-arched rim of 20 Országház Street; Baroque-like spirals above the twin windows*

The new palace bearing the marks of the Vienna Baroque style, a garrison-like building built by Maria Theresa, stood here as early as 1770 on the leveled-out, filled-up ruins of the palace from Matthias's era that was ultimately destroyed in 1686. But the last royal residence of Europe in which the king never stayed—except for a few days— was not truly finished until 1905. It was grandiose, bombastic and bleak.

129

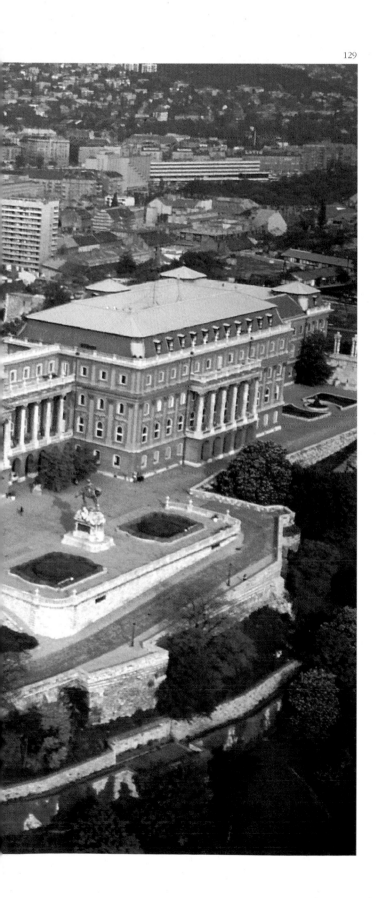

130

131

129. *The Royal Palace of Baroque Buda*
130. *The big bastion and the Palace*
131. *The southern Palace courtyard was the gala garden of the old palace of Matthias's era*

93

132. *Knight sporting a hat*
133. *Combed hair, groomed mustache, magnificent veiled high hat on the head: the knights of King Sigismund were worthy of the court; they kept pace with European fashion*
134. *Female head; the remnant of a 15th century corbel in Buda Palace*
135. *The chapel of the medieval palace*

The famed luxurious Gothic and Renaissance palace complex of Louis the Great, Sigismund and Matthias was destroyed in the blaze of sieges. Only what had been stolen or preserved under the soil remained of the architecture and arts of medieval Buda Palace. And sometimes the soil holds surprises. After 1945, a few buildings of old palaces were reconstructed, such as the Gothic assembly hall and the small chapel. And in 1974 archaeologists discovered a real sensation: a sculpture gallery. Royal court ladies, knights and their heralds, clergymen— once all gilded, colorfully painted. The 15th century court of Sigismund of Luxembourg came back to life.

The fate of Europe's largest Baroque/Neo-Baroque palace is a bit comic, or rather tragicomic. On a few occasions, Franz Joseph resided there, but he never governed the country from there. Then came the admiral-regent Miklós Horthy, statesmen in Hungarian gala dress, halberdiers, guards in Árpád helmets and white cloaks. A real wax museum. And what lay behind it: Trianon and two world wars.

136. *The gate of the ante-garden of the palace, ornamented in Baroque-like style*
137. *The fountain sculpture of the fishing boy*
138. *The Matthias Fountain, with the statue of the horseman driving his horse in front*

The Neo-Baroque palace was bombed in the winter of 1944-1945. The richly carved oak paneling was destroyed, as was the Zsolnay fireplace and the deep blue silk brocade wall covers with the crown and the cross woven into them, the paintings and the sculptures, the Saint Stephen and the Hunyadi rooms... Everything went up in flames like wood and cardboard theater scenery.

139. *The equestrian statue of Jenő Savoyai*
140. *The path along the Castle's eastern walls*
141. *The main facade of the palace*

142. *The palace in Buda Castle from the Chain Bridge*
143. *The palace with the Fishermen's Bastion and*
Matthias Church behind it, bathed in evening floodlights

The ornamented stairs of the Palace garden, Japanese garden and rock garden, and the garden pavilions were all destroyed; the past wanted to surface from beneath their ruins, from the depths of the soil. For these provided cover for the remnants of the fortress complex and the old palace. Today, the Baroque Royal Palace of Buda—for perhaps the first time in its history—finally has a worthy role as the citadel of Hungarian culture, housing museums, picture galleries and the national library.

Let's say farewell to Budapest with the lines of an ancient poet that still hold true today:
"Buda and Pest: two pages of
a lavish picture book
which the Danube divides, connects
and frames."
The poet, naturally, is a native and lover of Buda. We know only the date of his death: 1643. And his lengthy Turkish name: Vüdsudi Mehmed Ibnu-I-Abdu-l-Aziz.

145

144. *The night lights of the Chain Bridge, the row of street lamps on the Pest side of the Danube embankment in the background*
145. *Danube and the Chain Bridge and Budapest by night*

"Live, mortals, for as long as the Fates allow. Be a farmer, citizen, soldier or mariner, love Venus's flowers, open Ceres's blessed gifts, enjoy Minerva's plentiful and inspiring donations. Live a pure life cheerfully and with a just mind in your childhood and youth, then as a man and a tired elder. This way, even in your grave you will not be forgotten by those in the sky."
(From a Roman legionnaire's epitaph in Óbuda.)

146. *The sculpture of town-protecting Pallas Athene at the corner of the old City Hall of Buda*